CUTE COLORING BOOK

Inspirational Coloring Books

COLORING BOOKS FOR ADULTS

This Book belongs to

____

____

____

TEST YOUR COLOR

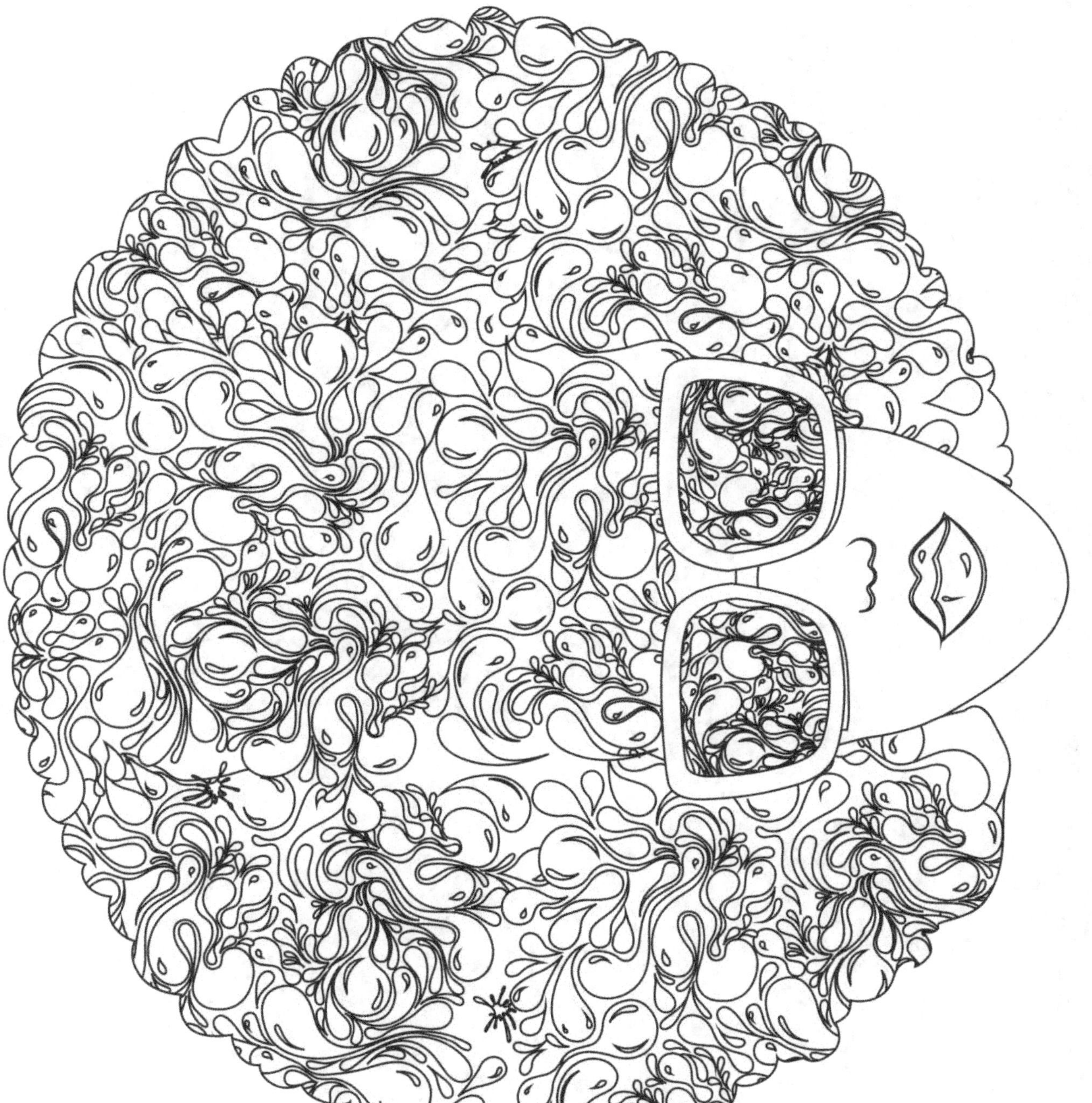

Kiss
love
Happy

WOW!
Brains!
BIG
CITY

DOODLES
I U
U ROCK!

BACK TO SCHOOL
BACK TO SCHOOL
EMAIL
BOOK
FILE
FUN
COLOR
RED
NOTE

monsters

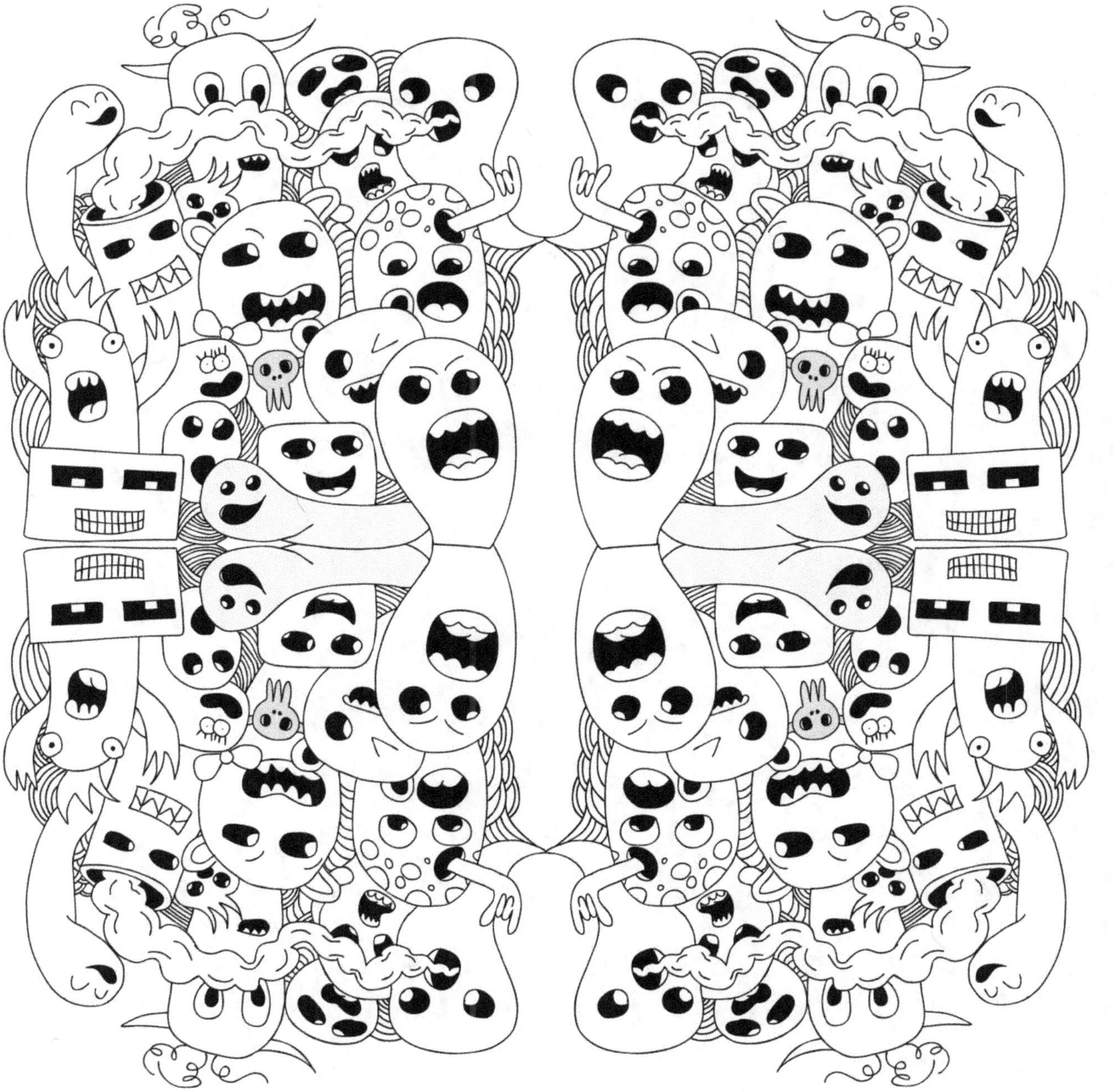

Social monster

YOUR tExt

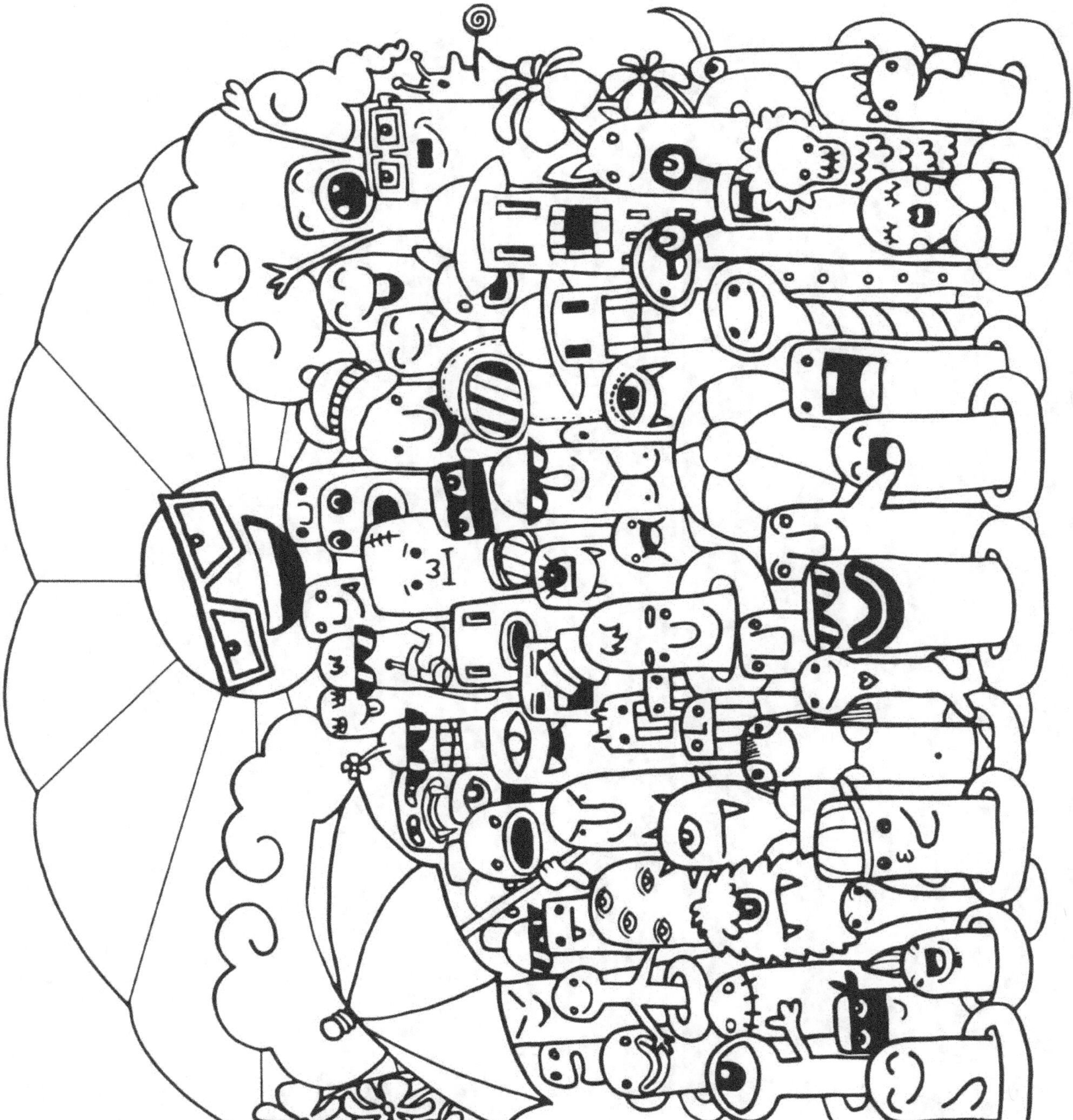

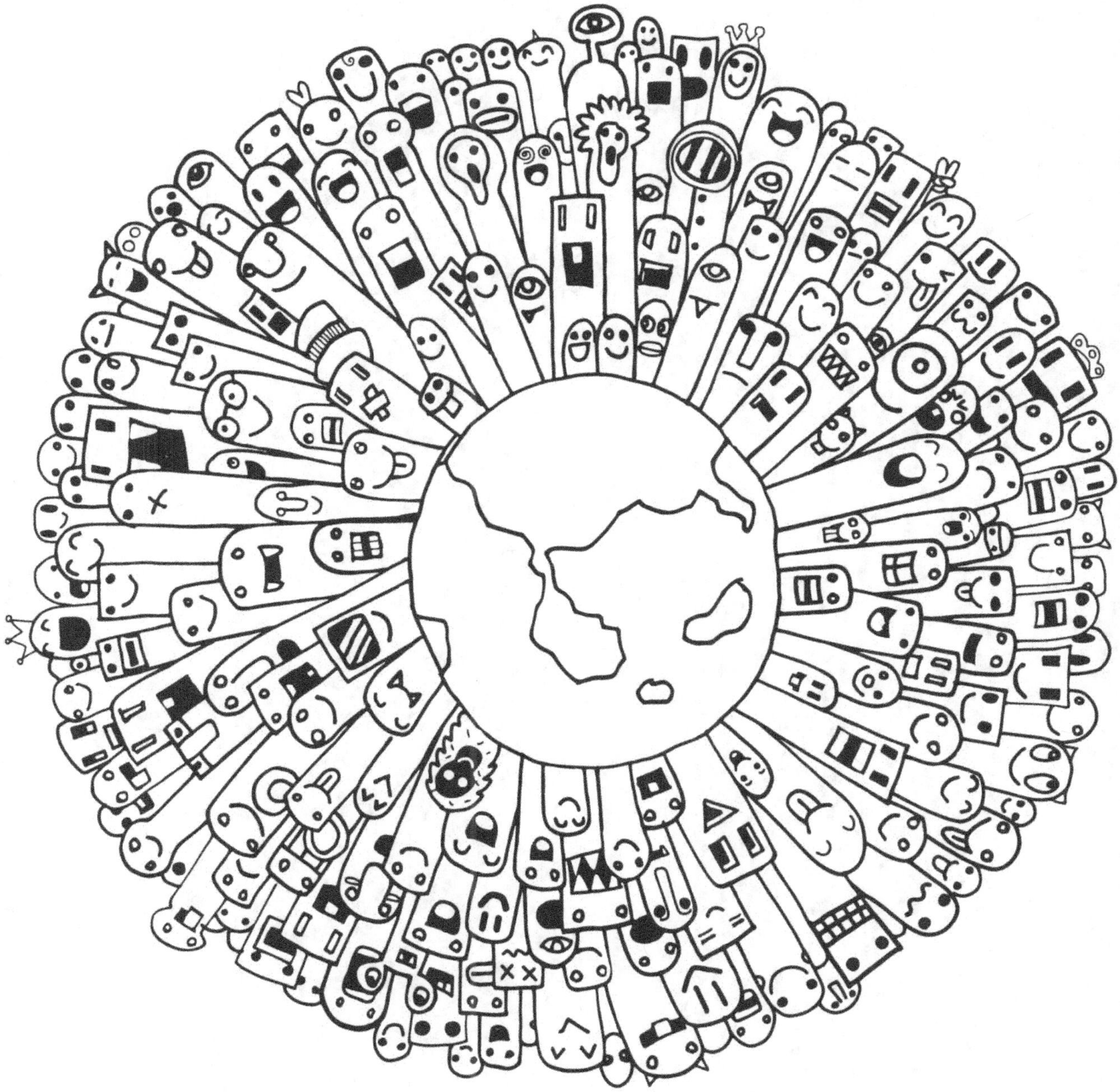

YOUR
TEXT

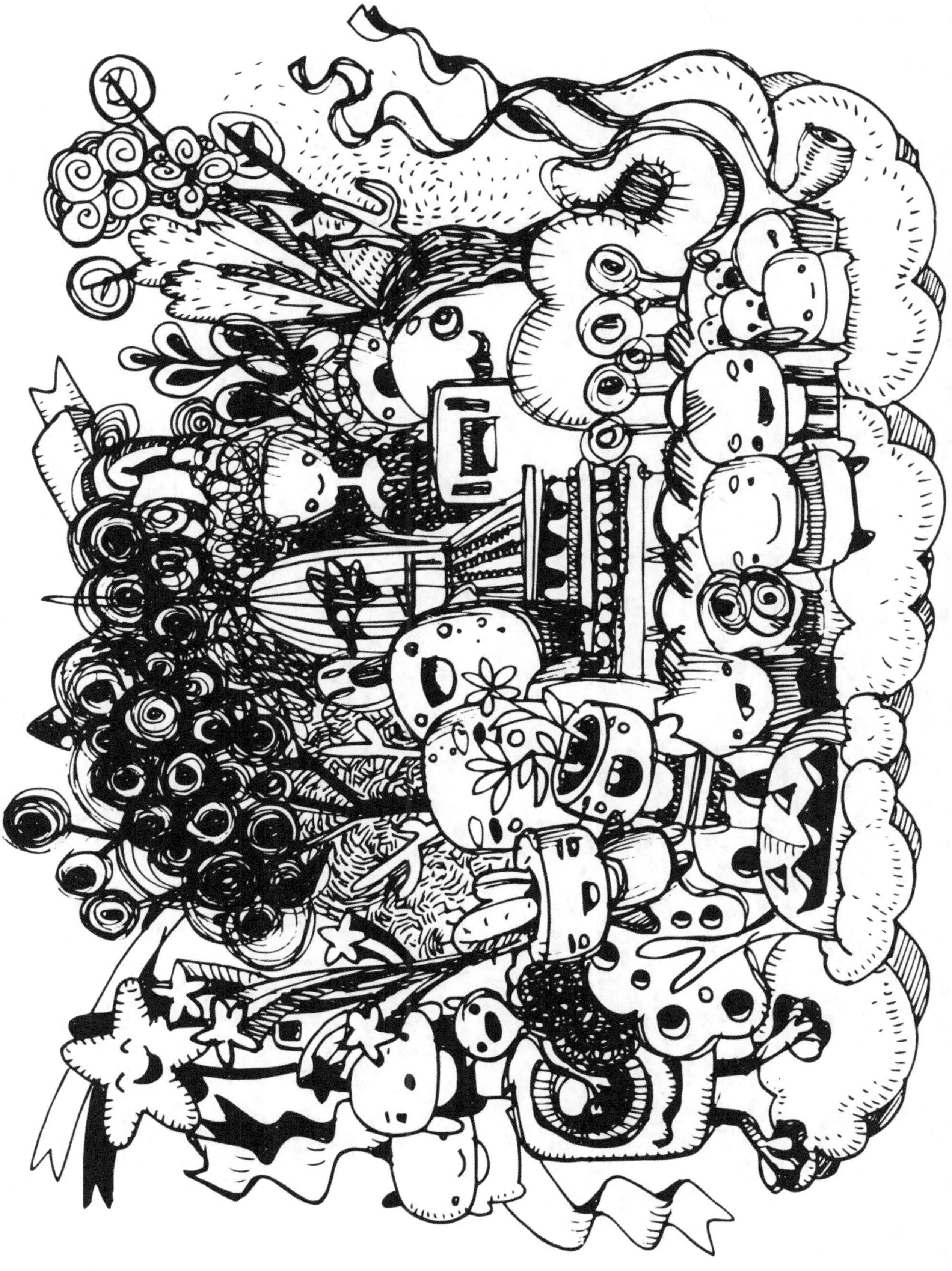

www.ingramcontent.com/pod-product-compliance
Lightning Source LLC
Chambersburg PA
CBHW081418280526
45788CB00009B/3141
* 9 7 8 1 5 4 3 0 0 8 9 4 4 *